About the book

There are 2 International GCSE Mathematics higher papers and answers in this book. These are papers 1H & 2H written as practice papers for IGCSE Mathematics Higher Examination. Papers are mainly focusing on Edexcel IGCSE examinations as well as other similar examination boards.

These papers are written according to the new grade 9-1 syllabus and questions are potential questions for the IGCSE mathematics examinations.

All the questions in this book are written by the author and they are new questions written purely to help and offer practice to students to prepare and test themselves for the IGCSE mathematics higher exams.

Solutions are included in this book. However, if you need to check your solutions, I advise you to ask your school mathematics teacher or your private mathematics tutor to mark your answers.

Both papers are calculator papers.

IGCSE Mathematics May/June 2024 Practice Papers

**for grade 9 to 1 syllabuses by Edexcel includes answers
Higher level**

By Dilan Wimalasena

Contents

Page

Practice Papers
Paper 1H   7
Paper 2H   17

Solutions
Paper 1H solutions   29
Paper 2H solutions   37

Paper 1H

Calculator Allowed
Time allowed 2 hours

1. Here are the first 4 terms of a sequence.

$$-1, 3, 9, 17, \ldots \ldots$$

Work out an expression for the nth term of the sequence.

(4 marks)

2. Work out the HCF & LCM of 126 & 210.

(4 marks)

3. A regular polygon has 15 sides. Work out the value of each exterior & interior angle of the polygon.

(3 marks)

4. David wants to invest £5500 over a period of 6 years. The bank offers 3.25% compound interest for the first 2 years and 1.99% compound interest after that. Calculate his balance at the end of the 6th year.

(3 marks)

5. Factorise the following expressions fully.
   i) $25a^2 - 16y^2$

(2 marks)

   ii) $4x^2 - 17x - 15$

(3 marks)
(total 5 marks)

6. Work out the following and write your answer in standard form.
   i) $(3.4 \times 10^{-7}) \times (1.5 \times 10^2)$

(2 marks)

   ii) $(1.8 \times 10^6) + (2 \times 10^4)$

(2 marks)
(total 4 marks)

7. Expand & simplify.

$$(2 - 5\sqrt{7})(5 + 2\sqrt{7})$$

(3 marks)

8. A bag has 6 red apples and 9 green apples. Neil picks two apples at random.
   i) Draw a tree diagram clearly showing all possible outcomes.

   (3 marks)

   Work out the probability of picking
   ii) Two green apples

   (2 marks)

   iii) One of each

   (3 marks)

   iv) At least one green apple

   (2 marks)
   (total 10 marks)

9. Work out the equation of the parallel line to $2y - 3x + 5 = 0$ through the point $P(3, -1)$.

   (4 marks)

11

10. Solve the following
   i) $3(4x - 3) - 5(2x + 7) = 2$

   (3 marks)

   ii) $-6 < 5x - 2 \leq 1$

   (3 marks)
   (total 6 marks)

11. A sphere has radius $6cm$. A cylinder with the same volume as the sphere has radius $3cm$. Work out the surface area of the cylinder.

   (5 marks)

12. Simplify the following.
   i) $\left(\dfrac{2x^2}{3y^7}\right)^3$

   (3 marks)

   ii) $(3a^3)^6 \times (2a^4)^2$

   (3 marks)
   (6 marks)

13. A computer is on sale for £651 after a 16% discount. Calculate the original price of the computer.

(3 marks)

14. $f(x) = 2x - 5$ & $g(x) = 3x + 1$.

   i) Work out a) $fg(x)$ & b) $g^{-1}(5)$

(5 marks)

   ii) Hence or otherwise, solve the following.

   $$fg(x) = g^{-1}(5)$$

(2 marks)
(total 7 marks)

15. Michael walked 1.8km in 12 minutes.
    i) Calculate his average speed in metres per second.

    (2 marks)

    ii) Convert his average speed to kilometres per hour.

    (2 marks)
    (total 4 marks)

16. The radius of the sector AOB is 10cm & the length AB is 6cm. Calculate the area of the shaded region.

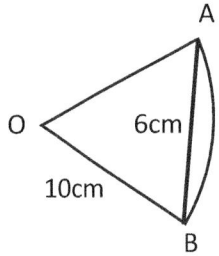

    (6 marks)

17. There are 60 people in a club. 45 play football and 34 play rugby. 7 people do not play neither.
    i) Represent the above in a Venn diagram.

    (3 marks)

    ii) What is the probability of person playing both.

    (2 marks)
    (total 5 marks)

18. $f(x) = x^2 - 3x - 4$. The curve $y = f(x)$, meets the x axis at A & B and the y axis at C.

    i)   Work out the coordinates of the points A, B & C.

(3 marks)

    ii)   The points A, B & C are mapped to the points P, Q & R by the transformation $y = 3f(x - 1) + 4$.
Work out the coordinates of the points P, Q & R.

(3 marks)
(total 6 marks)

19. Solve the following equation.
$$\frac{4}{x-4} - \frac{3}{x-2} = 3$$

(5 marks)

20. Draw a histogram for the following data.

Marks	Frequency		
20-30	2		
30-60	12		
60-70	12		
70-80	8		
80-100	3		

21. $2x^2 - 16x + 11 = a(x-b)^2 + c$.
Work out the values of a, b & c.

(4 marks)

The End
Total 100 marks

Paper 2H

Calculator Allowed
Time allowed 2 hours

1. Show that
$$3\frac{2}{5} \div \left(4\frac{1}{5} - 3\frac{1}{2}\right) = 4\frac{6}{7}$$

(4 marks)

2. A car has speed 86.4 km/h, and a train has speed 25 m/s. Which has the higher speed?

(3 marks)

3. $f(x) = 3x^2 - 10x - 8$
   i) Factorise $f(x)$ fully.

(3 marks)

   ii) Hence or otherwise, solve the equation $f(x) = 0$

(2 marks)
(total 5 marks)

4. Johannes, Kepler & Leroy shared £x in the ratio 3:7:10. Leroy has £126 more that Johannes. Work out the value of x.

(4 marks)

5. P is directly proportional to Q^2. When $P = 108, Q = -6$. Work out the values of
i) P when $Q = 10$

(3 marks)

ii) Q when $P = 147$

(3 marks)
(total 6 marks)

6. George wants to invest £150,000 in a savings account over a period of 10 years.

Bank Alpha offers	Bank Beta offers
3.99% compound interest	5.49% compound interest for the first 3 years & 2.49% compound interest for the remainder.

Which bank should he choose?

(4 marks)

20

7. Shade the region bounded by the following inequalities.

$$y < 2x + 1, \; y + 5x - 2 \leq 0 \; \& \; x > -1$$

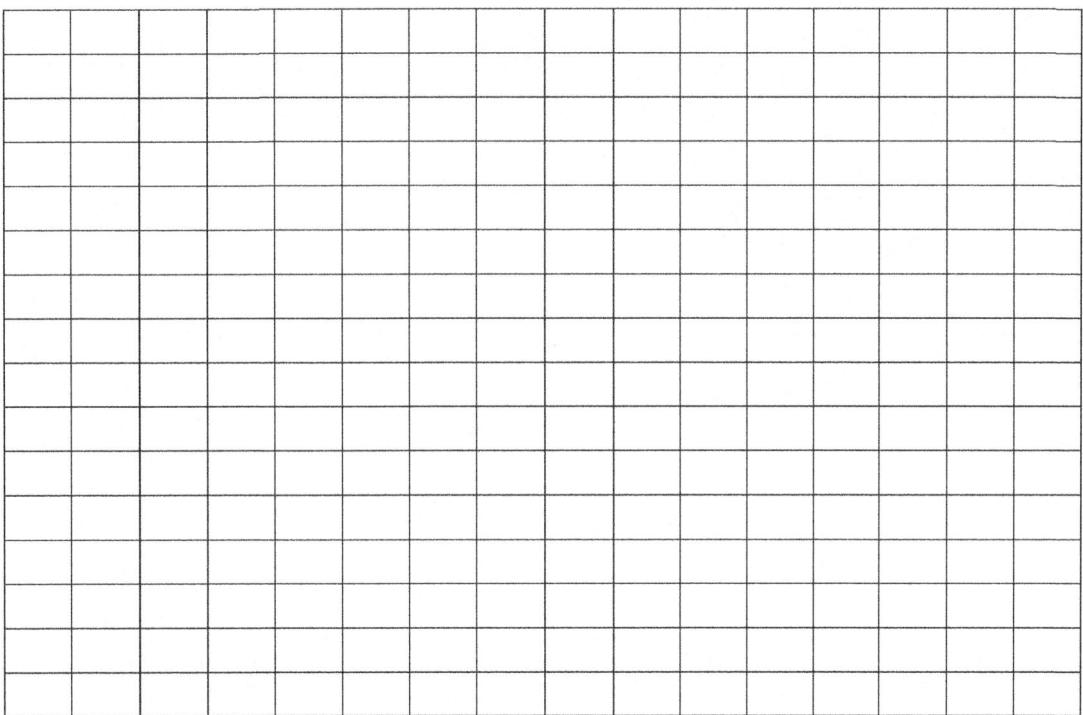

(4 marks)

8. Calculate the area of the shape below.

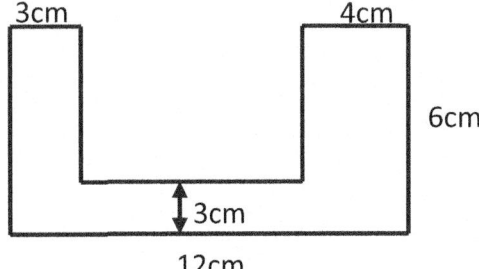

(3 marks)

9. Solve the following simultaneous equations.
   i) $2x - 7y = 25$
        $3x - 4y = 18$

(4 marks)

   ii) $ac = 54$
        $c - a = 15$

(4 marks)
(total 8 marks)

10. Calculate the area of the triangle ABC.

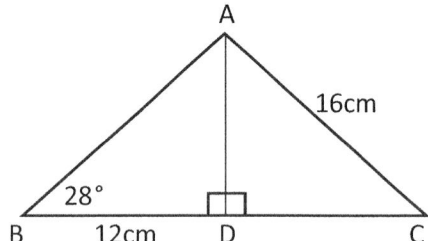

(6 marks)

11. The mean age of 3 people is 17. When the 4th person joins the group, the mean age is 15. How old is the 4th person?

(3 marks)

22

12. The table below shows data for heights of some students.

Height (cm)	Frequency
120-150	3
150-160	6
160-170	9
170-180	4
180-200	2

i) Draw a cumulative frequency curve.

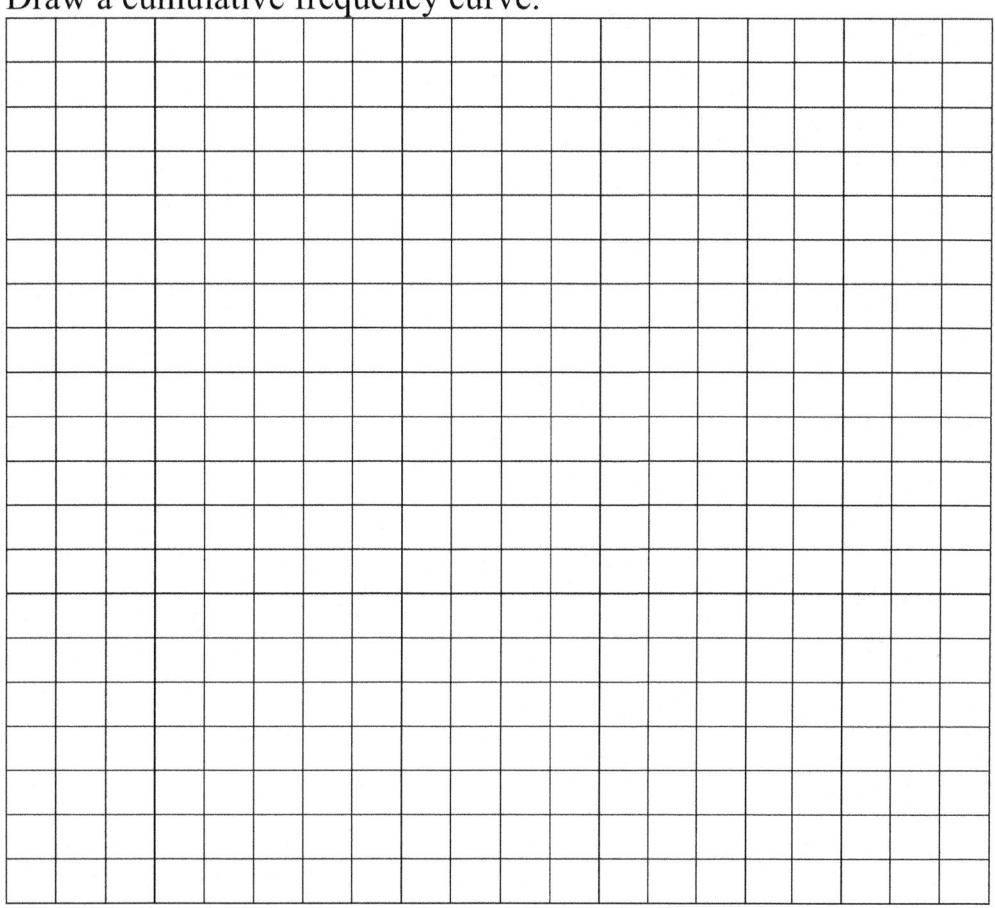

(2 marks)

ii) Work out the median height.

(2 marks)

iii) Work out the interquartile range.

(2 marks)
(total 6 marks)

13. Solve the following inequalities.

i) $\dfrac{2x-5}{3} \leq \dfrac{5}{6}$

(2 marks)

ii) $5x^2 - 7x - 6 > 0$

(3 marks)
(total 5 marks)

14. The radius of the circle shown is 6cm. Work out the area of the shaded region.

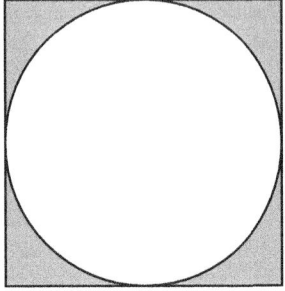

(4 marks)

15. There are 40 members in a sports club.
25 like archery, 15 like badminton & 20 like cricket.
5 like all three
6 like archery & badminton only
13 like archery and cricket
7 like badminton and cricket

i) Complete the Venn diagram for the data above.

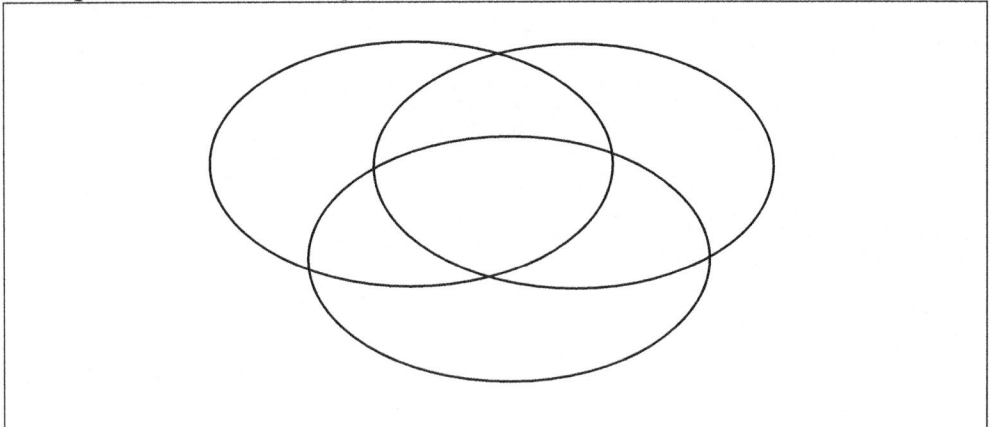

(3 marks)

ii) Work out the probability of a member not interested in any of the sports above.

(2 marks)
(total 5 marks)

16. *i*) Expand & simplify
$$(x+1)(2x-5)(2x+5)$$

(3 marks)

ii) Make q the subject of the formula.
$$p = \frac{a}{\sqrt{bq+c}}$$

(3 marks)
(total 6 marks)

17. The line l_1 has equation $3y - 6x + 9 = 0$. l_1 meets the x axis at A & the y axis at B.
  i) Work out the coordinates of the points A & B.

(3 marks)

  ii) Work out the distance AB in surd form.

(2 marks)
(total 5 marks)

18. Sketch the following curves.
  i) $y = \sin x$

(2 marks)

  ii) $y = \sin 2x$

(2 marks)
(total 2 marks)

19. Find the values of a & b.

$$\frac{5}{2x+3} - \frac{2}{3x-4} = \frac{ax+b}{(2x+3(3x-4)}$$

(4 marks)

20. $P = 1200 \ (correct\ to\ 2\ significant\ figures)$
    $Q = 25.6 \ (correct\ to\ 1\ decimal\ place)$

   i) Write down the upper and lower bounds for P & Q.

(2 marks)

   ii) Calculate the upper bound of the following to 5 significant figures.
   $$\left(\frac{PQ}{P-Q}\right)$$

(3 marks)
(total 5 marks)

21. OAB is a triangle. The vectors $\overrightarrow{OA} = 4a$ & $\overrightarrow{OB} = 4b$. The point C lies on OA such that $OC:CA = 3:1$. The point D is the midpoint of AB.

The line OB is extended to the point E. Given that the points C, D & E are colinear.

Work out the vector $\overrightarrow{BE}$.

(6 marks)

The End
Total 100 marks

Solutions 1H

1. $n^{th}\ term = an^2 + bn + c$

   $3 - (-1) = 4, 9 - 3 = 6, 17 - 9 = 8$

   $6 - 4 = 2, 8 - 6 = 2 \quad \therefore a = 1$

   $(-1, 3, 9, \ldots\ldots) - (1, 4, 9, \ldots\ldots) = -2, -1, 0, \ldots\ldots \quad \therefore b = 1\ \&\ c = -3$

   $so\ n^{th}\ term = n^2 + n - 3$

2. $126 = 2 \times 3 \times 3 \times 7$
   $210 = 2 \times 3 \times 5 \times 7$

   $HCF = 2 \times 3 \times 7 = 42$

   $LCM = 42 \times 3 \times 5 = 630$

3. Exterior angle $= \dfrac{360}{15} = 24°$

   Interior angle $= 180 - 24 = 156°$

4. Balance after first 2 years $= 5500 \times 1.0325^2 = £5863.31$

   Balance after 6 years $= 5863.31 \times 1.0199^4 = £6344.15$

5. i) $(5a + 4y)(5a - 4y)$

   ii) $4x^2 - 20x + 3x - 15$
   $= 4x(x - 5) + 3(x - 5)$
   $= (x - 5)(4x + 5)$

6. i) 5.1×10^{-5}

   ii) $(180 \times 10^4) + (2 \times 10^4)$
   $= 182 \times 10^4$
   $= 1.82 \times 10^6$

7. $2(5 + 2\sqrt{7}) - 5\sqrt{7}(5 + 2\sqrt{7})$
   $= 10 + 4\sqrt{7} - 25\sqrt{7} - 70$
   $= -60 - 21\sqrt{7}$

8. *i)* Draw a tree diagram with the following.

For the first pick, the red apples have a probability of $\frac{6}{15}$ & the green apples have $\frac{9}{15}$.

Assuming a red has been picked, then for the second pick reds have $\frac{5}{14}$ & greens have $\frac{9}{14}$. If a green has been picked first, then for the second pick reds have $\frac{6}{14}$ & greens have $\frac{8}{14}$.

ii) $P(g, g) = \frac{9}{15} \times \frac{8}{14} = \frac{12}{35}$

iii) $P(r, g) + P(g, r) = \left(\frac{6}{15} \times \frac{9}{14}\right) + \left(\frac{9}{15} \times \frac{6}{14}\right) = \frac{18}{35}$

iv) $1 - P(r, r) = 1 - \left(\frac{6}{15} \times \frac{5}{14}\right) = 1 - \frac{1}{7} = \frac{6}{7}$

9. $2y = 3x - 5 \quad y = \frac{3}{2}x - \frac{5}{2}$

$\therefore m = \frac{3}{2}$

$y = \frac{3}{2}x + c$ & when $x = 3, y = -1$

$-1 = \frac{3}{2}(3) + c$

$-\frac{2}{2} = \frac{9}{2} + c$

$-\frac{2}{2} - \frac{9}{2} = c$

$-\frac{11}{2} = c$

$y = \frac{3}{2}x - \frac{11}{2}$

10. i) $12x - 9 - 10x - 35 = 2$

$2x - 44 = 2$

$2x = 2 + 44$

$2x = 46$

$x = \dfrac{46}{2} = 23$

ii) $-6 + 2 < 5x \leq 1 + 2$

$-4 < 5x \leq 3$

$-\dfrac{4}{5} < x \leq \dfrac{3}{5}$

11. Volume of sphere $= \dfrac{4}{3}\pi(6)^3 = 288\pi \; cm^3$

Volume of cylinder $= \pi(3)^2 h = 9\pi h \; cm^3$

Height of cylinder $= \dfrac{288\pi}{9\pi} = 32 \; cm$

Surface area of cylinder $= 2\pi(3)^2 + 2\pi(3)(32)$

$= 18\pi + 192\pi$

$= 210\pi \; cm^2 \; or \; 659.73 \; cm^2$

12. i) $\dfrac{8x^6}{27y^{21}}$

ii) $3^6 a^{18} \times 2^2 a^8 = 729 a^{18} \times 4 a^8 = 2916 a^{26}$

13. Let x be the original price.

∴ $0.84 \, x = £651$

$x = \dfrac{£651}{0.84} = £775$

14. i) a) $fg(x)$
$= 2(3x+1) - 5$
$= 6x + 2 - 5$
$= 6x - 3$

b) let $y = 3x + 1$

$\frac{y-1}{3} = x$

$\therefore g^{-1}(x) = \frac{x-1}{3}$

$g^{-1}(5) = \frac{5-1}{3} = \frac{4}{3}$

ii) $6x - 3 = \frac{4}{3}$

$6x = \frac{4}{3} + 3$

$6x = \frac{13}{3}$

$x = \frac{13}{18}$

15. i) Average speed $= \frac{1800}{720} = 2.5 m/s$

ii) $2.5 \, m/s = \frac{2.5 \times 3600}{1000} = 9 \, km/h$

16. Angle AOB $= \cos^{-1}\left(\frac{10^2 + 10^2 - 6^2}{2(10)(10)}\right) = 34.9°$

Area of the sector $= \frac{34.9}{360} \times \pi(10)^2 = 30.46 \, cm^2$

Area of the triangle $= \frac{1}{2} \times 10 \times 10 \times \sin 34.9 = 28.61 \, cm^2$

Shaded area $= 30.46 - 28.61 = 1.85 \, cm^2$

17. *i*) F = Football & R = Rugby

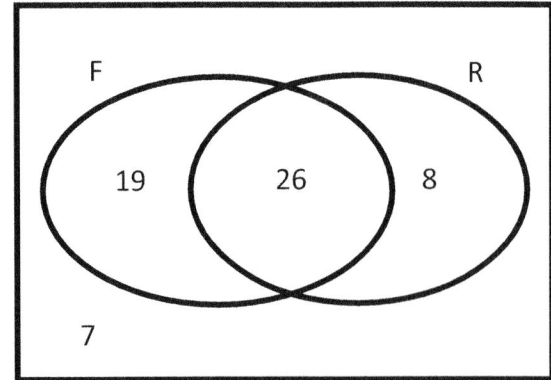

ii) $P(both) = \dfrac{26}{60} = \dfrac{13}{30}$

18. *i*) At A & B, $y = 0$, so $x^2 - 3x - 4 = 0$
$(x - 4)(x + 1) = 0$
$x - 4 = 0$ or $x + 1 = 0$
$x = 4$ or $x = -1$
$\therefore A(4,0)$ & $B(-1,0)$

At C, $x = 0$, so $y = -4$
$\therefore C(0, -4)$

ii) $P(5,4), Q(0,4), R(1, -8)$

19. Using common denominator
$\dfrac{4(x - 2) - 3(x - 4)}{(x - 4)(x - 2)} = 3$

$\dfrac{4x - 8 - 3x + 12}{x^2 - 6x + 8} = 3$

$x + 4 = 3(x^2 - 6x + 8)$

$0 = 3x^2 - 18x + 24 - x - 4$
$0 = 3x^2 - 19x + 20$
$0 = 3x^2 - 15x - 4x + 20$
$0 = 3x(x - 5) - 4(x - 5)$
$0 = (x - 5)(3x - 4)$
$x - 5 = 0$ or $3x - 4 = 0$
$x = 5$ or $x = \dfrac{4}{3}$

20. $Frequency\ Density = \frac{Frequency}{Class\ width}$

Marks	Frequency	Class width	Frequency density
20-30	2	10	0.2
30-60	12	30	0.4
60-70	12	10	1.2
70-80	8	10	0.8
80-100	3	20	0.15

Draw histogram with bars for each group with height frequency density.

21. $2x^2 - 16x + 11$
$= 2(x^2 - 8x) + 11$
$= 2[(x-4)^2 - 16] + 11$
$= 2(x-4)^2 - 32 + 11$
$= 2(x-4)^2 - 21$
$\therefore a = 2, b = 4\ \&\ c = -21$

Solutions 2H

1. Simplify the fractions using BIDMAS

$$\frac{17}{5} \div \left(\frac{21}{5} - \frac{7}{2}\right)$$

$$= \frac{17}{5} \div \left(\frac{42}{10} - \frac{35}{10}\right)$$

$$= \frac{17}{5} \div \frac{7}{10}$$

$$= \frac{17}{5} \times \frac{10}{7}$$

$$= \frac{17}{1} \times \frac{2}{7}$$

$$= \frac{34}{7} = 4\frac{6}{7}$$

2. Speed of the car $= \frac{86.4 \times 1000}{3600} = 24 \; m/s$

∴ The train is faster.

3. i) $3x^2 - 12x + 2x - 8$
   $= 3x(x - 4) + 2(x - 4)$
   $= (x - 4)(3x + 2)$

   ii) $(x - 4)(3x + 2) = 0$

   $x - 4 = 0 \; or \; 3x + 2 = 0$
   $x = 4 \; or \; x = -\frac{2}{3}$

4. 7 shares $= £126$

   1 share $= \frac{126}{7} = £18$

   Total shares $= 3 + 7 + 10 = 20$

   ∴ $x = £18 \times 20$

5. i) $P = kQ^2$

   when $P = 108, Q = -6$

   $108 = k(-6)^2$

   $108 = 36k$

   $\dfrac{108}{36} = k$

   $3 = k$

   $\therefore P = 3k^2$

   when $Q = 10$

   $P = 3(10)^2 = 300$

   ii) when $P = 147$

   $3Q^2 = 147$

   $Q^2 = \dfrac{147}{3}$

   $Q^2 = 49$

   $Q = \sqrt{49}$

   $Q = \pm 7$

6. Bank Alpha balance after 10 years $= 150{,}000 \times 1.0399^{10}$
   $= £221{,}823.24$

   Bank Beta balance after 3 years $= 150{,}000 \times 1.0549^3$
   $= £176{,}086.12$

   Bank Beta balance after 10 years $= 176{,}086.12 \times 1.0249^7$
   $= £209{,}168.16$

   $\therefore$ George should choose Bank Alpha.

7. Sketch the graphs of
$y < 2x + 1, y + 5x - 2 \leq 0$ & $x > -1$
And shade the regions defined by the inequalities.

8. Area A $= 3 \times 3 = 9m^2$
Area B $= 12 \times 3 = 36m^2$
Area C $= 4 \times 3 = 12m^2$
Total area $\quad 9 + 36 + 12 = 57m^2$

9.

$i)\ 2x - 7y = 25\ (1) \times 4$
$3x - 4y = 18\ (2) \times 7$
$8x - 28y = 100\ (3)$
$21x - 28y = 126\ (4)$
$(4) - (3)$
$13x = 26$
$x = \dfrac{26}{13} = 2$

Sub x into (2)
$3(2) - 4y = 18$
$6 - 4y = 18$
$6 - 18 = 4y$
$-12 = 4y$
$-\dfrac{12}{4} = y$
$-3 = y$

$ii)\ ac = 54\ (1)$
$c - a = 15\ (2)$
$c = a + 15\ (3)$
$Sub\ (3)\ into\ (1)$
$a(a + 15) = 54$
$a^2 + 15a - 54 = 0$
$(a + 18)(a - 3) = 0$
$a + 18 = 0\ or\ a - 3 = 0$
$a = -18\ or\ a = 3$

Sub a into (3)
when $a = -18$
$c = -18 + 15 = -3$
when $a = 3$
$c = 3 + 15 = 18$

10. $\tan 28 = \dfrac{AD}{12}$
$12 \tan 28 = AD$
$AD = 6.38 cm$

$CD^2 + 6.38^2 = 16^2$
$CD^2 = 16^2 - 6.38^2$
$CD = \sqrt{16^2 - 6.38^2}$
$CD = 14.67 cm$

$BC = 12 + 14.67 = 26.67 cm$

$$\therefore Area\ of\ \triangle ABC = \dfrac{26.67 \times 6.38}{2} = 85.08 cm^2$$

11. Total age of 3 people $= 3 \times 17 = 51$

    Total age of 4 people $= 4 \times 15 = 60$

    Age of the 4th person $= 60 - 51 = 9$ years

12. $i)$

Height (cm)	Frequency	Cumulative frequency
120-150	3	3
150-160	6	9
160-170	9	18
170-180	4	22
180-200	2	24

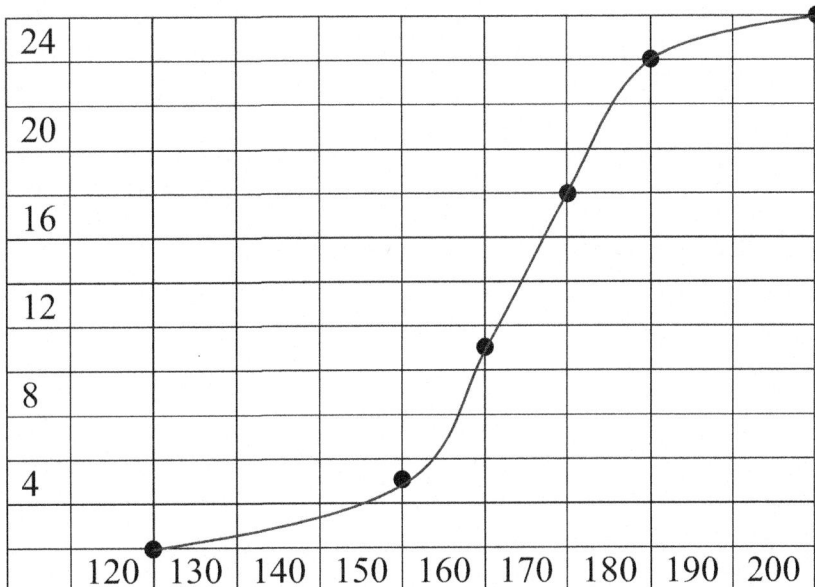

$i)\ median = \dfrac{24}{2} = 12^{th} = 164 cm$

$ii)\ Lower\ Quartile = \dfrac{1}{4} \times 24 = 6^{th} = 153 cm$

$Upper\ Quartile = \dfrac{3}{4} \times 24 = 18^{th} = 170 cm$

$Interquartile\ Range = 170 - 153 = 17 cm$

13. i)

$$6(2x - 5) \leq 15$$

$$12x - 30 \leq 15$$

$$12x \leq 15 + 30$$

$$12x \leq 45$$

$$x \leq \frac{45}{12}$$

$$x \leq \frac{15}{4}$$

ii)

$$5x^2 - 10x + 3x - 6 > 0$$

$$5x(x - 2) + 3(x - 2) > 0$$

$$(x - 2)(5x + 3) > 0$$

$$x < -\frac{3}{5} \, \& \, x > 2$$

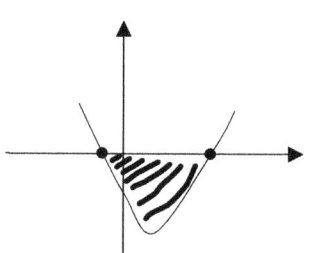

14. $Area\ of\ the\ cricle = \pi(6)^2 = 36\pi cm^2$

$Length\ of\ the\ square = 6 \times 2 = 12 cm$

$Area\ of\ the\ square = 12 \times 12 = 144 cm^2$

$\therefore Shaded\ area = 144 - 36\pi = 30.90 cm^2$

15. i)

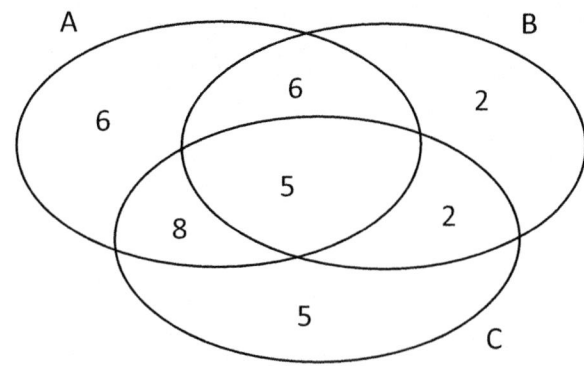

ii) $P(none) = \dfrac{6}{40} = \dfrac{3}{20}$

16. i) $(x+1)(4x^2 - 25)$

$= x(4x^2 - 25) + 1(24 - 25)$

$= 4x^3 - 25x + 4x^2 - 25$

$= 4x^3 + 4x^2 - 25x - 25$

ii) $p^2 = \dfrac{a^2}{bq + c}$

$p^2(bq + c) = a^2$

$p^2 bq + p^2 c = a^2$

$p^2 bq = a^2 - p^2 c$

$q = \dfrac{a^2 - p^2 c}{p^2 b}$

17.i)

$$at\ A, y = 0 \qquad\qquad at\ B, x = 0$$

$$-6x + 9 = 0 \qquad\qquad 3y + 9 = 0$$

$$9 = 6x \qquad\qquad 3y = -9$$

$$\frac{9}{6} = x \qquad\qquad y = -\frac{9}{3}$$

$$\frac{3}{2} = x \qquad\qquad y = -3$$

$$\qquad\qquad\qquad\qquad B(0, -3)$$

$$A\left(\frac{3}{2}, 0\right)$$

ii) $AB = \sqrt{\left(0 - \frac{3}{2}\right)^2 + (-3 - 0)^2}$

$= \sqrt{\frac{9}{4} + 9}$

$= \sqrt{\frac{9 + 36}{4}}$

$= \sqrt{\frac{45}{4}}$

$= \frac{3\sqrt{5}}{2}$

18. i) $y = \sin x$

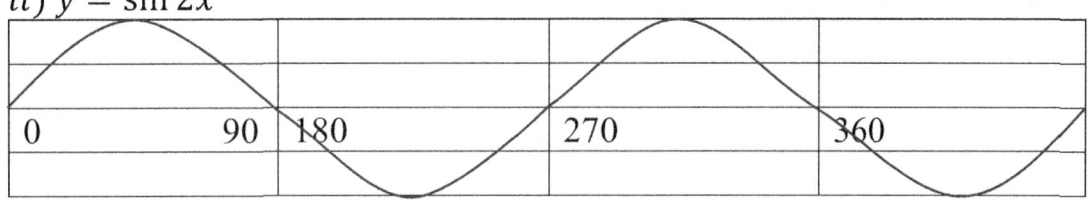

ii) $y = \sin 2x$

19. simplify using common denominator

$$\frac{5(3x-4) - 2(2x+3)}{(2x+3)(3x-4)}$$

$$= \frac{15x - 20 - 4x - 6}{(2x+3)(3x-4)}$$

$$= \frac{11x - 26}{(2x+3)(3x-4)}$$

$\therefore a = 11 \ \& \ b = -26$

20. i) $1150 \leq P < 1250 \ \& \ 25.55 \leq Q < 25.65$

ii) $\left(\dfrac{PQ}{P-Q}\right)_{upper} = \dfrac{(PQ)_{upper}}{(P-Q)_{lower}} = \dfrac{P_{upper} \times Q_{upper}}{P_{lower} - Q_{upper}}$

$$= \frac{1250 \times 25.65}{1150 - 25.65}$$

$= 28.516$

21. $\overrightarrow{AB} = \overrightarrow{AO} + \overrightarrow{OB}$
$= -4a + 4b$
$= 4b - 4a$

$\overrightarrow{CA} = \dfrac{1}{4}\overrightarrow{OA} = a$

$\overrightarrow{AD} = \dfrac{1}{2}\overrightarrow{AB} = 2b - 2a$

$\overrightarrow{CD} = \overrightarrow{CA} + \overrightarrow{AD}$
$= a + 2b - 2a$
$= 2b - a$

Let $\overrightarrow{BE} = kb$
then $\overrightarrow{OE} = \overrightarrow{OB} + \overrightarrow{BE}$
$= 4b + kb$
$= (4 + k)b$

$\overrightarrow{CE} = \overrightarrow{CO} + \overrightarrow{OE}$
$= -3a + (4 + k)b$
$= (4 + k)b - 3a$

since C, D & E are on a straight line $\overrightarrow{CD}$ is parallel to $\overrightarrow{CE}$

so $\dfrac{4 + k}{-3} = \dfrac{2}{-1}$
$4 + k = 6$
$\therefore k = 6 - 4 = 2$
So $\overrightarrow{BE} = 2b$

Printed in Great Britain
by Amazon